COLLAGE COUTURE STUDIO
paper dolls

Julie Nutting

NORTH LIGHT BOOKS
CINCINNATI, OHIO
createmixedmedia.com

CONTENTS

MATERIALS LIST

Surfaces

- 8" × 8" (20cm × 20cm) wrapped canvas
- 8" × 10" (20cm × 25cm) canvas or canvas board
- 11" × 14" (28cm × 36cm) canvas board
- 11" × 14" (28cm × 36cm) chipboard
- assorted scrapbook papers

Pigments/Acrylic Paints

- assorted

Brushes

- assorted

Other Supplies

- 1" (3cm) wooden ball knobs, 4
- 3D adhesive dots
- 3D metallic paint: brown, green, Royal Blue
- adhesive
- baby wipe
- binder rings, 2
- black distress ink pad
- black marker
- black pen, fine-point
- brads, 6 small and 2 large
- brown bag, small
- bubble wrap, small
- assorted buttons
- cardstock: blue, brown
- chalk-ink edgers: brown and dark brown
- chipboard book, chipboard scrap
- colored paper, brown or black
- colored pencils: assorted including 3 browns, red
- crackle medium
- craft glue

- crochet lace and trim
- assorted decorative papers
- decorative paperclip, small
- decoupage medium
- die cuts: angel wings, crown, dresses, fairy wings, flowers, mannequins (3), mini-tags, owl, purses, shoes, ticket
- doilies: white and colored
- double-sided tape
- dowel rod: ⅛" (3mm) and another size (optional)
- assorted embellishments
- foil adhesive paper
- gesso
- glimmer mists: brown, coral, yellow
- glitter glue, blue
- glossy accents embellishment glue
- glue stick
- hair dryer or heat gun (optional)
- heavy gel medium
- hole punch, ¼" (6mm)
- ink pads: black, red
- iridescent modeling paste
- markers: brown, gold, light yellow
- metal number
- metal photo corner holder
- mini-clothespins, 4
- modeling paste
- mulberry paper with gold thread
- painter's tape, ½" (1cm)
- palette knife
- paper distresser
- paper oval frame
- pencil
- punchinella

- rhinestone trim
- ribbon: black, brown, pink
- rubber stamps: Asian characters, assorted, flower-shaped, script
- rub-on metal paint, gold
- ruler
- sand
- sandpaper
- scalloped circle punch, 1" (3cm)
- scissors: regular and scalloped
- scrapbook paper doilies: brown, green, white
- sea sponge
- sewing machine
- shadow box, 8" × 10" (20cm × 25cm)
- Sharpie marker, black fine-point
- stationery box
- stencils: allover flower, cherry blossom branch, chicken wire, floral, leaf, linen weave, reverse chicken wire
- string
- threads: pink, red
- tulle, cream-colored
- washi tapes: script and travel-themed
- water spritzer
- white snow floral picks
- wooden box, 6" × 4½" × 1" (15cm × 11cm × 3cm)
- wooden clothespins with a crackle finish, 2

createmixedmedia.com/ paper-dolls

INTRODUCTION

In 2008, when I created my first mixed-media, faceless, paper-collaged doll made of newspaper, it was all about the fashion illustration. Fashion illustration has been a passion of mine since the age of nine. Little did I know then that the faceless darlings would become a successful book, stamp and craft product line. The direction of my art has taken a sharp, unintentional turn. Yes, it's still about the clothes, but it became more than that.

After teaching many classes on how to make my collaged dolls, I noticed it wasn't so much the techniques that the students were into. In fact, most people could teach me a thing or two and they have. Class after class we labored over backgrounds, which really wasn't too different from other classes out there. But then there was a sudden transformation in the room as I saw people of all ages finding their inner child as they chose just the right paper for a dress, cut a contrasting pocket or added the perfect bow for the hair. There would be complete silence as everyone contemplated the outfits. Should the dress be a floral or a check? Leggings would be cute! Headband or flower? Yep, these are serious decisions!

Then you'd hear squealing and maybe a giggle or two. Someone always shouted out that it's like playing paper dolls again. And didn't we all play with paper dolls? As children, we spent hours with these delightful, inexpensive toys. I would use the folders the dolls came in as their houses. A playmate would outline her paper-doll houses with toilet paper and get in trouble with her mom for wasting all that paper. Paper dolls were our companions through measles, mumps and chicken pox. They went to the hospital with us when we had our tonsils out. You could easily buy them at the corner drugstore. They were always a coveted party prize.

Those were simpler times, and the dolls gave us such joy. This book is about reconnecting with that joy. You don't have to wait for a rainy day or a sick day. Grab a cup of your favorite tea, your scissors and start cutting! The dolls in this book are meant to be cut out, used in your mixed-media art or scrapbooks. I hope the projects in this book will unleash your creativity and that you will find once again that child who loved playing with paper dolls. Although these were not designed for child's play, you certainly can use them to introduce a special little one to the art of playing paper dolls.

Tip

To make the most of Emilee and her friends, you may want to consider photocopying the dolls and clothes in this book. I'd recommend printing on cardstock, or print on regular printer paper and then adhere that to cardstock with decoupage medium or glue stick. The **Design Your Own Clothes** templates and other templates can also be photocopied, or visit createmixedmedia.com/paper-dolls for printable PDFs.

You will now meet some of the cutest paper girls from fashion capitals all over the globe. They have their own unique styles as you will find out when you see their darling wardrobes. Each girl has her place in the fashion world and her very own story to tell; some of their stories trace back centuries. Has it ever occurred to you to make up stories for your artwork as you're creating it? I believe this is what makes my creative time so much fun. Doing so truly turns my art time into playtime!

With each girl you will find dresses, coats, pants, skirts and tops as well as some pretty, adorable accessory pieces. After all, what's a girl without her accessories? Everything is meant to mix and match so you can create a bunch of different outfits for each girl. You can easily turn a classic outfit into something funky simply by adding striped leggings and, oh, I don't know, maybe a giant polka-dot bow in her hair! If you feel you're missing something, you'll find some simple patterns to make the outfit of your choosing. Craft stores are filled to the brim with tons of coordinating papers that work perfectly to make a wardrobe all your own.

I hope you have as much fun playing paper dolls as I do. You may even want to change their stories! Emilee, from New York, may become a beach babe from Miami or Belle could easily be a feisty little senorita from Barcelona!

We will start out in New York City with Emilee as she travels to four amazing cities. We'll visit London, Paris, Florence and Tokyo to meet four of Emilee's best friends. Have fun as you follow their adventures!

EMILEE

I'd like to introduce Emilee. She is from New York City and her mom is an agent in the fashion business, so they get to travel all over the world together. Emilee has a strong sense of style and hers is a bit bohemian with a little hippie thrown in. Her style fits right in with the atmosphere of her funky neighborhood, which is filled with coffeehouses, vintage shops and art galleries. She also loves vivid gypsy colors and adores anything hand-embroidered or quilted. She loves to hunt down vintage clothing in some of the shops near her home, and she enjoys taking classes to learn how to crochet and embroider.

Her favorite things: coffee (whenever she can sneak it), hats, crochet classes, purple, the zoo, cupcakes with purple frosting, scrapbooking her travels and tea at The Plaza.

createmixedmedia.com/paper-dolls

CHARLEY

This is Charley. She's from London and lives in a flat overlooking the Thames. She loves to look out at Big Ben at night before she goes to sleep. It makes her think of pixie dust and flying off to magical make-believe places. She's a bit of a dreamer and loves to sit and read classics from old leather-bound books that her grandmother collected as a small girl. On a gray, mist-filled day, you can find her curled up reading an old, yellowed copy of *The Secret Garden*.

Charley's mom owns one of the largest modeling agencies in the world. Her grandmother was one of Britain's top models in the 1960s. Yep, she was a part of the miniskirt, frosted lipstick and long, fake eyelash days. The look has definitely influenced Charley. She likes anything that screams mod, from geometric prints to white go-go boots.

Her favorite things: fairies, books, puppies, puddle jumping without an umbrella, scouring flea markets, scones without raisins, hot pink, vintage umbrellas and anything sixties.

BELLE

Off to Paris to meet Belle. Ah, yes, the City of Light, where her family has been a part of the fashion world since the 1920s, when her great-great grand-mère was a tailor for a very famous designer we all know and love. Her tailoring skills were exquisite and she handed them down to future generations, keeping Belle's family in the fashion business ever since. They live in the outskirts of Paris in a château surrounded by gardens as beautiful as Giverny itself. She is often found in the garden dressed in her girly frills, having tea with make-believe princesses.

Her style is classic French: impeccable workmanship, clean lines and with a few ruffles thrown in for good measure. Anything pink, vintage lace or menswear stripes with an updated touch can be found in her closet.

Her favorite things: pink, castles, tiaras, kittens, bubble baths, raspberry macaroons, fairy gardens, shopping the streets of Paris and hunting for vintage lace, trims and buttons.

FRANCESCA

We make a quick stop in Italy to meet the darling Francesca. She's a bit of a tomboy, loving all things leather and denim. Yes, you guessed it. Her family has owned a leather business since Renaissance times. They have clothed some of the most famous Europeans in history from their beautiful little village tucked away in the hills of Tuscany.

She is quite the artist, influenced by some of the greatest museums right down the road. You can usually find her somewhere outside painting the beautiful countryside. She loves to spend time in the old family factory, finding leather scraps to paint on and then having them made into small bags or wallets.

Although she's most comfortable in denim and T-shirts, she loves the old-world look of tapestries, damask and rich earth tones that mark the more romantic times of centuries past. You will also find ruffles and cabbage rose prints in her vast wardrobe.

Her favorite things: paint, lemon gelato, biscotti, old and grungy leather boots, old maps, vintage Venetian lace, art museums and wandering the cobblestone streets of old Florence in search of the perfect place to paint.

KYOKO

Our final destination is Tokyo where we meet Kyoko. Kyoko's family has owned a silk factory for a very long time. They have sold to the couture market in Europe for decades and make the finest silk in all of Japan. Kyoko's father brings her bags of silk scraps, which she fashions into some of the most colorful, crazy Harajuku styles. The less the fabrics match, the more she likes the finished piece. Her clothes are crazy fun just like her personality!

She lives in a large, traditional Japanese-style home on the outskirts of the big city. She loves day trips to the city where she can rummage through secondhand shops to find vintage kimonos and old pieces of colorful silk. Then off for tea in a traditional teahouse where she orders her favorite honey cakes.

Her favorite things: vintage silk, origami animals, afternoon tea, paper lanterns in bright colors, old parasols, jump rope and sketching anime girls with big eyes.

createmixedmedia.com/paper-dolls

2 Design Your Own Dolls and Clothes

Get Creative!

I learned how to draw when I was about nine by tracing my paper dolls and drawing their clothes. I colored them in with crayons, colored pencils and markers. I spent hours doing this and I still do!

I thought it would be fun for you to design your own dolls and clothes. In this chapter you will find clothing templates for each doll so you are not limited to the outfits I created. In addition to these, there is a doll template without a face or hair so you can create your very own! She has several outfit templates so you can mix and match until there's no tomorrow!

You can trace these patterns onto decorative papers to create your paper dolls, or you can use plain white cardstock. They can then be colored in with professional-style illustration markers or a good-quality colored pencil. You can create any kind of hairstyle you want and that might even include pink pigtails! I give you permission to go crazy with these templates! Your clothes may be customized for the holidays, school colors or modeled after a favorite dress.

I'm sure these dolls will find their way into many projects. Whether it's through canvas art, cards or scrapbook pages, I know you will have hours of fun creating your own paper dolls.

EMILEE

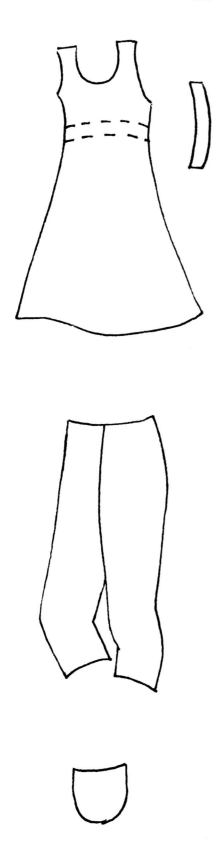
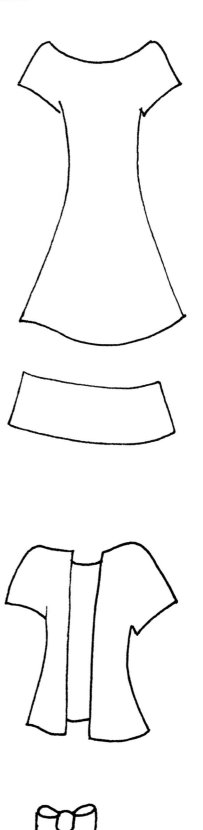

KYOKO

Design Your Own Doll Template

createmixedmedia.com/paper-dolls

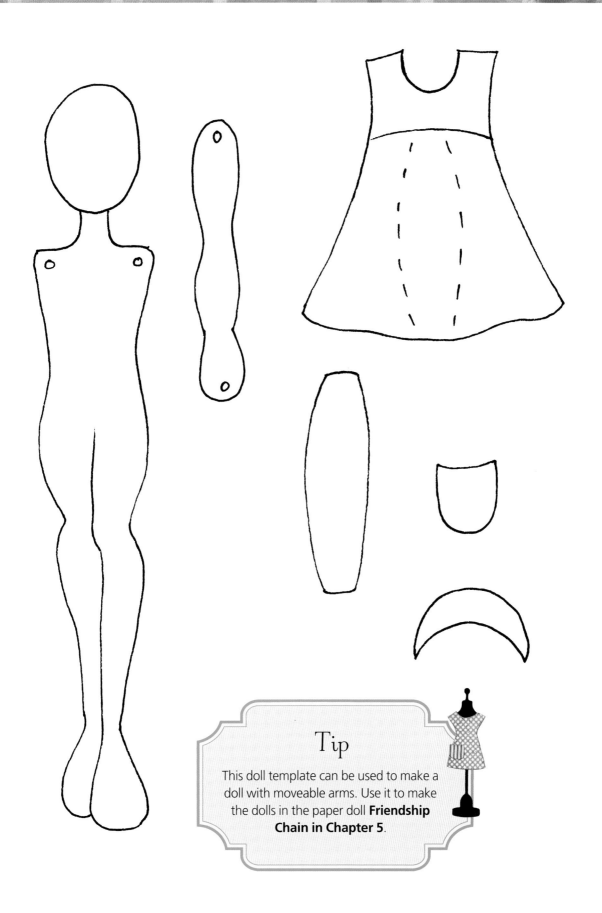

Tip

This doll template can be used to make a doll with moveable arms. Use it to make the dolls in the paper doll **Friendship Chain in Chapter 5**.

3

Paper Doll Settings

Let's Play Paper Dolls!

When I was a child, paper dolls came in a chipboard folder. The folders were always beautifully illustrated to match the theme of the dolls. Do you remember those? I used to stand the folders up all throughout the living room while playing and they became my dolls' homes. In my wonderful world of mixed-media art, my paper dolls need their own wonderful handmade settings. You can apply a chipboard easel back to stand them up or simply place them on plate stands to create a paper doll village! I can imagine giving a group of backgrounds to a young girl with a set of paper dolls to play with.

These can also be used as a backgrounds onto which to decoupage paper dolls, creating lovely paper doll art. I have photo ledges in my studio and I arrange my settings on them with paper dolls placed in front. I can change things according to the season or my mood. That way I always have an excuse to play and make new dolls!

We will be using an array of mediums to create these pieces using some very basic mixed-media techniques. You will probably have most of the supplies on hand if you are an avid crafter. You can adapt these projects to any canvas size you please.

Emilee Goes to the Beach

Of course, living in New York City can be hectic and crazy sometimes. That's why Emilee's family has a beach house where they spend their summers!

I love torn paper and use it quite often when I create. I use this technique for my gowns and I thought it would also make a wonderful ocean. Keep in mind that the more irregular the torn papers are, the more interesting the art will be.

I used a sand paint that is readily available from many manufacturers, or you can create your own by simply mixing clean sand with white glue. There is something magical about using seashells, pearls and gems together. The mixture reminds me of a trove of treasures that a mermaid princess might possess hidden far beneath the sea!

MATERIALS LIST

11" × 14" (28cm × 36cm) flat canvas board

acrylic paints: white, lime green, turquoise, light blue, medium, brown, green

adhesive

brown chalk-ink edger

decoupage medium

glitter glue: blue

metallic 3D paint: brown, green, royal blue

paintbrushes

pearls and rhinestones

pencil

sand

scissors

scrapbook paper in a variety of browns, blues and greens

seashells

sea sponge

water spritzer

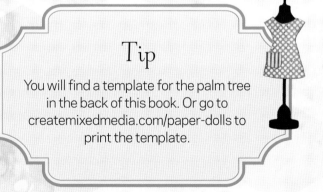

Tip

You will find a template for the palm tree in the back of this book. Or go to createmixedmedia.com/paper-dolls to print the template.

1 Drizzle white paint on the canvas. Paint light blue into the white and spread it all over the canvas. Add more paint as needed.

2 Add a little lime green and turquoise and randomly mix them into the blue background until it pleases you. Be careful not to overmix the paints. Allow the paint to dry.

Tip

Use a heat gun or hair dryer to speed up the drying process.

3 Wet a sea sponge, dip it in white paint and gently daub it on the top of the canvas to create clouds. If the paint is too thick, spritz the canvas with water and keep daubing.

4 Sponge in a bit of the lime green, light blue and turquoise. Blend as desired. Then sponge in a bit of medium brown in the top corners. Allow to dry completely.

5 Rip about five pieces of brown and sandy-colored scrapbook paper into ½" to ¾" (13mm-19mm) strips. These strips should be uneven in order to create a pleasing texture.

6 Decoupage the strips in layers across the bottom of the canvas to create the sand of the beach. Push out any air bubbles with your fingers before the strips dry. The sand should cover about 3" to 4" (8cm-10cm) of the bottom of the canvas.

7 Rip blue and green papers into strips. Use a variety of shades and patterns to create the ocean. Decoupage the first green or blue strip about 7½" (19cm) from the top of the canvas. Don't start near the sand. Leave the white rip marks at the top of each layer to simulate the crest of waves.

8 Before the decoupage medium dries, roll back the white crests to create three-dimensional waves at the top of each layer. Continue adding layers and pulling back the crests until you reach the brown sand.

Layer a coat of decoupage medium over the collaged elements to seal the paper. This is a good time to push out any remaining air bubbles.

Tip

Feel free to leave the white edges of the ripped paper showing for added texture and interest. To get the white tear marks, rip the paper towards you, pulling up the design on the front of the page.

9 Trace palm tree leaves onto green paper, cut them out and ink the edges. Do the same for the trunk using brown paper.

10 Place the palm tree on the right side of the board and adhere it using decoupage medium. The trunk should be about 1" (3mm) from the bottom of the canvas. Adhere the palm leaf to the top of the palm tree to give it dimension. Cover the entire board with a layer of decoupage medium to seal it.

11 On the trunk of the tree, squiggle brown metallic 3D paint to give the tree dimension. Use green metallic 3D paint to do the same for the leaves. Allow some of the squiggles to go off the paper and onto the canvas.

12 Drizzle royal blue 3D metallic paint onto the sky.

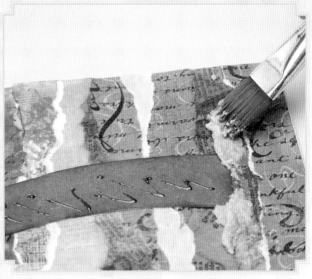

13 Mix sand with decoupage medium to create a sandy glue adhesive.

14 Spread the sand mixture at the base of the palm tree for texture and across the bottom of the background in random spots.

Tip

You can buy sand paint instead of making your own.

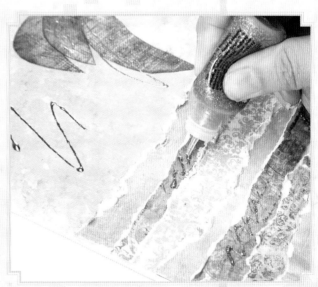

15 Embellish the base sand with real seashells, paper starfish, pearls, rhinestones and other beach-themed décor.

16 Squiggle blue glitter glue in random places across the waves.

There's no place like home. Home sweet home. Home is where the heart

46

The House on Cherry Tree Lane

When I was young I had a large picture book that I bought at my school's book fair. It was the story of that famous English nanny we all have come to love. I remember a page in the book where that nanny was landing in the neighborhood she would soon be working in. The houses in this particular book had lots of lacy iron fretwork, and bubblegum-pink cherry trees throughout the landscape. I had always wished I lived in a neighborhood that was predominantly bubblegum-pink!

Now, I know Charley lives in a city flat in London and I'm sure it's pretty nice, but I'm thinking she secretly wishes she lived in a colorful London neighborhood inhabited by flying nannies and filled with bright pink cherry trees! Who wouldn't?

When I decided to do a house for my paper dolls, of course this favorite page from my childhood book came to mind. I had a piece of scrapbook paper that featured those yummy candy hues and the horizontal scallops were perfect for the roof. The roof could also be composed of different strips of colored papers with edges decoratively punched. Make sure you use your prettiest embellishments to give your house curb appeal!

MATERIALS LIST

8" × 10" (20cm × 25cm) canvas or canvas board

acrylic paint: light blue, white, red, royal blue, raw umber, medium brown

black pen, fine-point

brown and green scrapbook paper doilies

brown chalk-ink edger

buttons

decoupage medium

gesso

hair dryer or heat gun (optional)

metal number

assorted scrapbook papers, green tones

paintbrush

scalloped circle punch, 1" (3cm)

small bubble wrap

striped scrapbook paper, 2 kinds

wooden door

1 Paint a coat of light blue acrylic paint over the canvas board. Gently feather in white acrylic paint in random places. Be careful not to overmix.

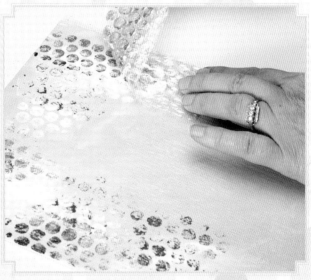

2 Use bubble wrap to apply random bits of white, royal blue and red paint.

3 Tear several pieces of green scrapbook paper into 8" (20cm) long strips of varying widths. Using decoupage medium, apply these strips in layers, beginning 3" (8cm) from the bottom and working down. The final piece should be the bottom piece.

4 Cut a 5" × 5½" (13cm × 14cm) piece of striped scrapbook paper. Ink the edges using a brown chalk-ink edger. Apply it to the center of the canvas about ½" (1cm) from the bottom using decoupage medium. Cut a complementary piece of a different striped paper into the shape of a roof that is about 3½" (9cm) tall. Cut a brown scrapbook paper doily into a small tree shape. Ink the edges. Apply the tree so that it peeks out from behind the right side of the roof (the roof should overlap the house by 1¾" or 4cm). Use decoupage medium to secure both.

5 Using decoupage medium, add a small scalloped piece of paper to the top of the roof for added interest (create your own design with the scallop punch). Apply a wooden door to the center of the house and place a 1½" (4cm) square window (teal paper) on both sides. Embellish the windows with a slightly smaller square of patterned paper applied with decoupage medium. Allow to dry.

6 Drybrush gesso lightly over the whole piece, including the sky, house, door and green hills.

7 Paint a basic/primitive tree trunk with raw umber acrylic paint on the right side of the house. Highlight the tree with a light to medium brown.

8 While the tree is drying, glue bright paper circles on both sides of the house. Glue stacks of colorful buttons onto the circles.

Tip

You can use a die-cut doily for the trees in any patterned paper you choose!

9 Using a fine-point black pen, draw stems on the flowers, scallops under the roof and a saying along the roofline. Attach the green paper doily above at the top of the tree, overlapping the roof slightly. Glue a number on the roof of the house.

paris

The City of Light

Ahhh, yes. Of course I had to include the beloved Eiffel Tower in my paper doll settings. I, like most American crafters, am enamored with this structure. Just the sight of it evokes dreams of romance, images of delicious food, wondrous architecture and strolling down boulevards lined with amazing shops.

Because my little Belle is oh so feminine, I just had to make this setting in a very Parisian black and white with a hint of sugary pink. As I embellished, I thought a little lace and sparkle never hurt a girl.

When working with all the gorgeous scrapbooking papers available, I really study the compositions to see what elements of that paper I can use in my work. For this piece, I cut out the pink roses from one paper and the word *extraordinaire* (which I thought would be charming to use in this piece) from another. See what you may find within your papers to create your own one-of-a-kind masterpiece.

I put this piece in a very simple but elegant frame, thinking it would be perfect sitting in an ornate plate stand, looking very French indeed. I also think this would make a very elegant card with a paper doll off to the side.

MATERIALS LIST

11" × 14" (28cm × 36cm) chipboard
11" × 14" (28cm × 36cm) frame
assorted embellishments
assorted paper flowers
black scrapbook paper
brown and coral Glimmer Mists
brown chalk-ink edger
chicken wire stencil
decorative ribbon
dowel rod (optional)
Eiffel Tower template

floral stencil
gesso
glossy accents embellishment glue
glue stick
assorted French-themed patterned scrapbook papers
paintbrushes
punchinella
rhinestone trim
scissors
white paper doily

Tip

You will find a template for the Eiffel Tower in the back of this book. Or go to createmixedmedia.com/paper-dolls to print the template.

1 Glue two pieces of scrapbook paper, 11" × 9" (28cm × 23cm) and 11" × 5½" (28cm × 14cm), to a piece of chipboard (or the frame backing). The bottom piece should overlap the top piece slightly. Glue a piece of decorative ribbon across the seam to hide it.

2 Trace the Eiffel Tower template onto black paper. Cut it out and set it aside. Find some decorative elements on a piece of scrapbook paper and cut them out. Ink the edges using brown chalk-ink edger.

Tip

You can find all sorts of hidden treasures or decorative bits on pieces of scrapbook paper. Just cut them out and use them in your compositions!

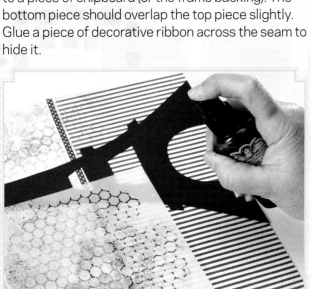

3 Glue the Eiffel Tower and the decorative paper elements to the paper background using a glue stick. Lightly spritz brown Glimmer Mist through the floral stencil in random places. Spritz coral Glimmer Mist through the chicken wire stencil in random areas.

4 Drybrush gesso in random areas. Then place a punchinella in other random areas and drybrush more gesso.

5 Cut a paper doily to match the width of each floor on the Eiffel Tower. Glue them down with a glue stick and cover the seams with rhinestone trim glued down with glossy accent embellishment glue.

6 Cut a piece of black patterned scrapbook paper into a 5" (13cm) circle. Cut the circle into a coil.

7 Starting with the center end, wrap the coil around a dowel rod or paintbrush. Using tacky glue, glue the wrapped paper to the outside end of the coil. As the glue dries, the rose will spread out naturally. Allow it to dry thoroughly.

8 Attach the black rose to the left side of the Eiffel Tower and embellish the rest of your piece with flowers, ribbons, rhinestones, charms, mini Scrabble tiles that spell *Paris*, etc.

Pagoda in the Park

I have always been a fan of origami paper and small Asian trinkets. Living close to San Francisco as a kid will do that to you. I couldn't wait to go into those shops in Chinatown with hundreds of little treasures lining the aisles. Pure delight for any child! When I came across this small 6" × 6" (15cm × 15cm) pad of Asian-themed paper, I was quickly reminded of those shops with rows of hanging lanterns, paper parasols, beautiful origami paper and a whole trove of other goodies.

A pagoda was a natural choice for a paper-doll setting for Kyoko. I set to work cutting these pretty little papers and couldn't wait to use modeling paste with a new cherry blossom stencil I had just purchased. Stamping with bubble wrap is always a welcome addition to mixed-media work.

MATERIALS LIST

8" × 10" (20cm × 25cm) canvas board

Asian-themed scrapbook paper

acrylic paint: light yellow, light pink, magenta

brown chalk-ink edger

bubble wrap

cherry blossom branch stencil

craft glue

decoupage medium

embellishments: buttons, rhinestones, metal trinkets, charms and paper flowers

gesso

Glimmer Mist: coral, yellow, brown

heat gun or hair dryer (optional)

heavy gel medium

iridescent modeling paste

pagoda template

paintbrushes

painter's tape, ½" (1cm) wide

palette knife

punchinella

scissors

Tip

You will find a template for the pagoda in the back of this book. Or go to createmixedmedia.com/paper-dolls to print the template.

1 Paint a basecoat of light yellow acrylic paint. Allow it to dry.

2 Using ½" (1cm) wide painter's tape, create a sunburst pattern in the top right corner of the canvas board.

Tip

To speed up the drying process use a hair dryer or heat gun on a low setting.

3 Paint a layer of light pink paint onto the bubbly side of bubble wrap, then press the paint onto the board in random areas until there is no paint left on the bubble wrap.

4 Between the pieces of tape, apply a layer of heavy gel medium mixed with yellow paint. Mix in a bit of magenta paint as well until the color pleases you. Allow this to dry thoroughly.

createmixedmedia.com/paper-dolls

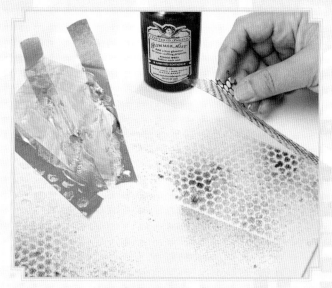

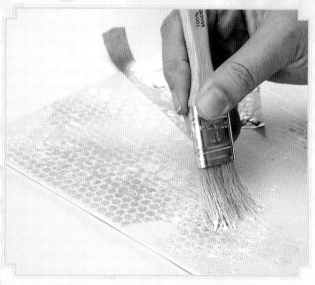

5 Place a piece of punchinella in the upper left corner of the canvas and spritz it lightly with coral Glimmer Mist. Do the same in the bottom right corner. Allow it to dry.

6 Drybrush a layer of gesso in random places on the canvas.

7 Trace the pagoda template on a piece of scrapbook paper. Trace the smaller pagoda pieces on a different piece of scrapbook paper. Cut out all the pieces.

8 Ink the edges of the pagoda with the brown chalk-ink edger.

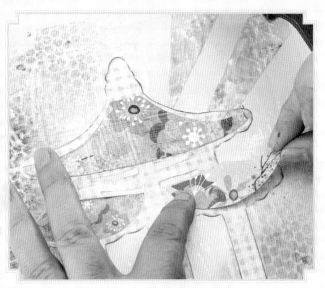

9 Carefully remove the painter's tape from the sunburst.

10 Decoupage the pagoda in the center of the canvas and about ½" (1cm) from the bottom edge. Add the smaller decorative pagoda papers to the roof using decoupage medium.

Layer the decoupage medium over the entire board. The Glimmer Mist will smudge a bit and that is OK. Allow these elements to dry.

11 Place the cherry-blossom branch stencil in the upper left corner of the pagoda and the canvas. Spread modeling paste over the stencil using a palette knife. Carefully remove the stencil. Repeat in a small portion of the right center. Allow the modeling paste to dry.

12 Attach buttons, paper flowers, rhinestones, metal trinkets and charms in the bottom corners (the more texture, the better!). I lay them out first to see how I want the arrangement to look. Once the arrangement is pleasing to you, glue the embellishments down.

13 Cover the embellishments with gel medium. Allow this to dry.

14 Drybrush gesso in random places over the embellishments. Spread the gesso in places where you want Glimmer Mist to stick.

15 Spray the embellishments with coral Glimmer Mist, a bit of yellow Glimmer Mist and a small amount of brown Glimmer Mist. Allow the yellow and coral to dry before adding the brown.

16 Add the final flower to the top center of the pagoda using craft glue.

Paper Couture Shoppe

I had completed all the projects for this book when I spotted the most delicate dress-form die at my local stamp store. I had to have it! What better way to use it than for a dress shop window display! So once again I set about finding the perfect papers for my little shop. I had every intention of doing a traditional striped canopy, but when I spotted this hexagon paper in the yummiest of candy-colored hues, I knew this would be my shop canopy. I must admit, I had so much fun designing and cutting out these tiny outfits. I knew instantly this would have to go into this book because every paper doll needs a place to shop! This will sit on a picture ledge in my studio with one of my paper dolls standing nearby.

MATERIALS LIST

3D glue dots

11" × 14" (28cm × 36cm) canvas board

acrylic paints: cream, red, white, teal, medium brown, green

baby wipes

brown chalk-ink edger

craft glue (double-sided tape, optional)

chipboard bird

decoupage medium

doily, small white

embellishments: small half wooden flowerpot, paper flowers, buttons, wire daisies, stone stickers

ink pad, black

Glimmer Mist: coral

lace or ribbon

mannequin die cuts, 3

modeling paste

paintbrushes

pencil

punchinella

rub-on metal paint, gold

rubber stamp, flower shaped

scissors

scrapbook papers of your choice

stencils: flower, linen weave, reverse chicken wire

water spritzer

1 Paint an 11" × 14" (28cm × 36cm) canvas board with a basecoat of cream acrylic paint. Don't let it dry completely.

2 Mix white with teal paint to create a very light teal color. Brush thin amounts of teal into the cream background and add water to create a water-color effect. Use a baby wipe to blend the paints. Repeat in a few random areas of the canvas.

3 Using a darker teal, paint the flower stencil near the edges of the canvas in random spots. Use very little paint to create a subtle effect. Allow it to dry.

4 Place the punchinella in random places and lightly paint it with white paint and a dry brush.

Tip

Protect your work surface from the Glimmer Mist by covering it with a scrap of paper or spraying over a trash can.

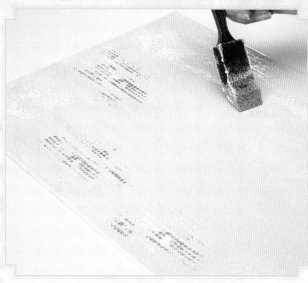

5 Using medium brown paint, paint over the linen weave stencil in random locations. Allow the paint to dry.

6 Cover the whole canvas with a layer of decoupage medium.

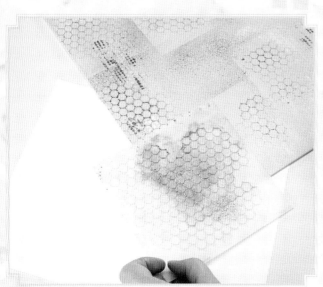

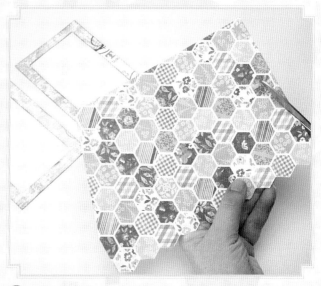

7 Place the reverse chicken wire stencil in random places and spray with coral Glimmer Mist.

8 Cut two rectangles 5½" × 3½" (14cm × 9cm) from scrapbook paper. Cut out the inside to create a ½" (1cm) thick frame. Cut an 8¼" × 6" (21cm × 15cm) rectangle from a second piece of paper. Trim the sides at an angle to create the awning for the shoppe roof.

Tip

Choosing paper with an all-over pattern such as hexagons gives you the opportunity to cut a pretty edge to your awning piece.

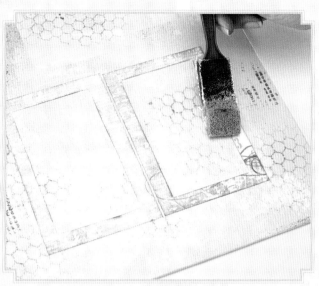

9 Score a horizontal line about 1" (3cm) from the top of the awning, and fold it toward you. At the bottom of the paper, score a line about 1½" (4cm) from the bottom and fold the flap down and away from you.

10 Adhere the frames (now becoming your storefront windows) using decoupage medium approximately 2" (5cm) from the bottom of the canvas. The interior edges of the frames should meet in the center of the canvas. Cover the frames with decoupage medium to secure them to the canvas.

11 Cut a small white doily in half and attach it to the top of each window frame with decoupage medium. Be sure to leave enough room in the frames for the mannequin stands.

12 Trace three dress shapes on paper, following the curves of the mannequin die cuts. Cut out the dresses from scrapbook paper and ink the edges with a brown chalk-ink edger.

13 Adhere the mannequin shapes inside of the windows. The left window will get two mannequins (one higher than the other to show depth), and the right window will get one, closer to where the frames meet. Apply dresses to the mannequins with decoupage medium.

14 Add a 1¾" × 2" (4cm × 5cm) sign to the right frame. I found scrapbook paper that had a sign preprinted, or you can make a custom sign.

15 Position the awning above the windows, making sure the doilies peek out. Adhere the top folded edge using craft glue or double-sided tape.

16 Cut a piece of lace that is the length of the top of the awning and glue it with craft glue to hide the seam.

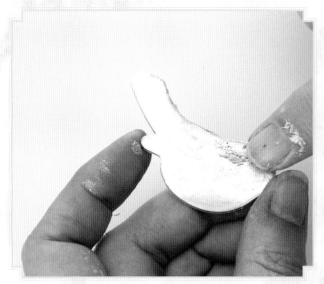

17 Using your finger, rub gold rub-on paint on the chipboard bird. Add a hint of green paint to the belly area of the bird. Use your finger to rub a hint of red paint onto the bird's back. Blend the paints until the bird is pleasing.

18 Embellish the bird with a stamp of your choosing. Adhere the bird to the top left corner of the awning using a glue dot.

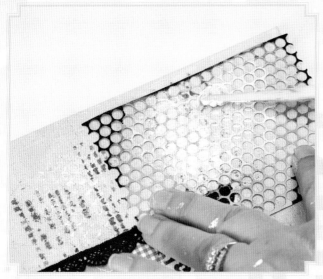

19 Place the punchinella randomly near the top of the canvas and apply cream-colored modeling paste. Apply more modeling-paste punchinella marks to the bottom center of the canvas to simulate steps leading to the doors of your shoppe.

20 Embellish the bottom left corner of the canvas. Paint the half flowerpot red. Arrange the flowerpot and flowers in the corner and adhere.

Tip

Spritz the flowers with water, scrunch them up and then unscrunch them to make the petals look more natural. Use buttons for the centers of the flowers. Wrap the wire stems of three wire daisies around a dowel rod or pencil to make them cute and curly. Arrange them, using plenty of glue, in the flowerpot in a pleasing arrangement.

21 Ink a flower-themed rubber stamp and apply it to the bottom of the canvas in a couple of random spots. Then arrange flowers in the right corner and glue them down. Adhere stone stickers to the center of each door frame for doorknobs.

4

Flea Market Finds

Let's Go Shopping!

Who wouldn't want to go to a flea market while traveling abroad? I would love to have a friend in every country who could show me the ins and outs of all the vintage marketplaces. I love scouring around for vintage goodies wherever I travel. It's just part of my routine, so I thought that would be a fun addition for the paper dolls.

In my paper-doll world the girls visit some of the best flea markets around the world and find all kinds of goodies to alter and repurpose. Made from old stationery boxes, wood boxes and just good old-fashioned paper, these fun projects became delightful places where I could stash the dolls' clothes and accessories. I hope you become inspired to find all sorts of ways to create storage for your dolls and their wardrobes.

First Stop ... London Antique Shops

Just look what Emilee and Charley found while scouring the secondhand shops of London. This beautiful old room screen was sitting in front of a little country antique store. It needed sprucing up, but it became the perfect piece for Emilee to decorate her boho-themed bedroom.

When I began this project, I had a folding three-sectioned room screen in mind, something that could stand on display while storing some of my paper doll supplies I have waiting to go into projects. As the project progressed, I saw a wonderful card idea emerging. Imagine receiving a card like this from a special friend, complete with a paper doll and dresses tucked in the pocket with perhaps a sweet message. Hmmm … I see some great holiday projects stemming from this!

MATERIALS LIST

- 8" (20cm) piece of pink rayon ribbon
- alphabet stickers
- assorted paper and fabric flowers
- baker's twine
- craft glue
- craft tape
- decorative edge punch
- embellishments: leaf, architectural details

- faux wood scrapbook paper
- glue stick
- paper clip, decorative
- paper doll
- paper distresser
- scissors
- variety of double-sided floral scrapbook papers
- washi tape

1 Cut two 6" × 12" (15cm × 30cm) pieces of double-sided floral scrapbook paper. Score a line 4" (10cm) from the bottom and fold up. Distress the flaps with a paper distresser.

2 Cut two pieces of decorative paper that have been punched at the top, 2" × 6" (5cm × 15cm) long. Glue them to the back of the distressed flap using a glue stick. Distress the top even more by peeling it back so you can start to see the pattern on the reverse side. Repeat on the second piece.

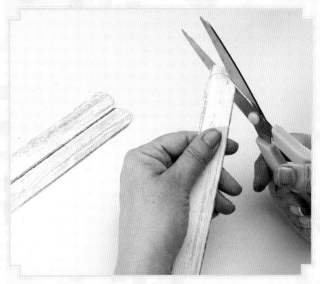

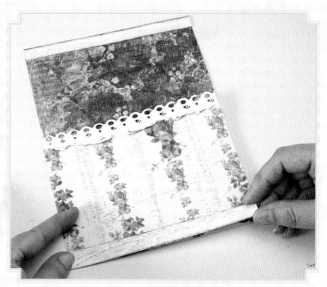

3 Cut four 2" × 10 ½" (15cm × 27cm) strips from the faux wood paper. Fold them in half lengthwise. Cut a half circle at the top of the each and a quarter circle curve at the bottom of each to make legs. These will be the support posts for the screen frame.

4 Cut eight ½" × 6" (1cm × 15cm) strips of faux wood paper. Ink the edges. Glue a wood strip on the top and the bottom of the flapped panel. Repeat on the back of the panel and on the second flapped panel.

5 Adhere the support posts around the left and right sides of both flapped panels using a glue stick, aligning the bottom curve with the bottom edge of the screen. This will create pockets from the flaps. The very tops and bottoms of these posts should be adhered to each other.

6 Hinge the two panels of the screen together using 1" (3cm) strips of washi tape. Flip the screen over and add a second set of washi tape hinges for added security.

Fold the screen so the pockets are on the inside facing each other. Resecure the posts with more glue if needed.

Tip

When you are cutting the small rounded shapes, use an emery board to file the curve and make it a smooth, round shape. Ink the edges of each post (both sides).

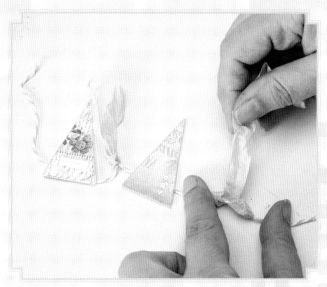

7 Create a banner with three scrapbook paper diamonds folded and glued around a piece of baker's twine to create triangle flags. Leave space between each flag to tie a ribbon. Cut the 8" (20cm) ribbon in half and tie a piece between each flag.

8 Lay the banner across the top front of the screen. Glue the middle triangle flag to the panel with a dot of craft glue. Glue the other triangles down around the middle triangle.

Tip

Scrunch the ribbon into a ball and spray it with water to make it look vintage.

9 Create another banner by cutting a 1¼" × 3½" (3cm × 9cm) piece of paper. Cut a **V** at the bottom of the banner. Ink the edges. Write *For You* on the banner with alphabet stickers and clip it to the top panel using a decorative paper clip. Embellish the bottom right-hand corner with paper and fabric flowers and a leaf adhered with craft tape.

10 Open the screen. Glue an architectural embellishment to the inside, positioning it so it sticks up from the top and can be seen when the screen is closed. Slip a paper doll in one of the pockets.

The Famous Flea Markets of Paris

Who could travel to Paris without visiting some of the flea markets it's so famous for? Well, that's just how Emilee and Belle decided to spend a glorious day in vintage heaven! As they rummaged through dozens of old, musty armoires, Emilee finally found the perfect piece to ship home and restore.

I wanted an armoire that reeked of sugary, pink Parisian goodness in which to stash my paper dresses! How fun would it be to take this a step further and make hatboxes, hats and other goodies to stash inside!

This armoire is simply a box that small notecards came in. It was a pretty pink color, so I didn't have to cover the entire box, which made this project very easy; I am always on the lookout for simple things to make something beautiful out of! The base is a wooden plaque that can be purchased at any craft store for under a dollar.

MATERIALS LIST

acrylic paint: medium brown and cream

assorted scrapbook paper

brown chalk-ink edger

chipboard

crackle medium

craft glue or glue stick

decorative paper with doily pattern

embellishments: die-cut purses, shoes, dresses, etc.

foil adhesive paper

paintbrushes

paper oval frame

sandpaper

stationery box

wooden pieces: 2 decorative dollhouse moldings, 5 knobs (4 legs and 1 doorknob), base, flower – all sized to fit the size of stationery box you've chosen

1 Paint all of the wooden pieces with medium brown acrylic paint. Allow the pieces to dry.

2 Paint a coat of crackle finish on all of the wood pieces. Allow the finish to dry until tacky.

3 Cover each wooden piece with a layer of cream paint. Watch the crackle layer take effect! Allow all the pieces to dry thoroughly.

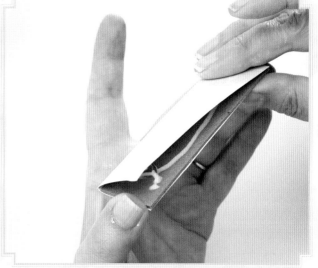

4 Cut a piece of chipboard to the width and depth of the inside of the box. Cover the chipboard with decorative paper. Glue it and let dry.

5 Cut a piece of decorative paper to fit the inside of the box. Adhere it using a glue stick.

6 Cut a piece of wood molding to size. Glue it inside the box about a third of the way down from the top to create the base for a shelf.

7 Glue the covered chipboard to the top of the molding to create a shelf. Allow to dry.

8 Cut out two doilies from patterned papers. Cut each doily in half.

9 Ink the edges of three of the halves with a brown chalk-ink edger.

10 Glue the three halves to the top of the inside of the box to create a decorative curtain. Retain the remaining half for later.

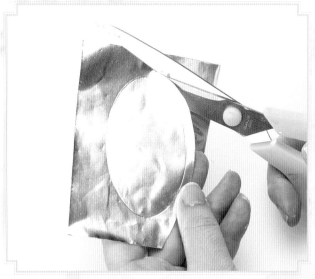

11 Cut a piece of foil adhesive to fit behind a die-cut oval, scalloped frame.

12 Glue the foil piece to the frame to create a mirror.

createmixedmedia.com/paper-dolls

13 Glue the mirror to the inside of the box door.

14 Embellish the inside of the armoire with die-cut accessories like purses, shoes and dresses.

Tip

You can buy adorable accessory stickers such as handbags and hats to decorate the inside of your armoire.

15 Cut decorative paper to fit the front outside and the back outside of the box (about 1/8" [3mm] smaller all around than the actual size). Ink the edges of the paper and adhere one piece to the front and one to the back.

Cut two more pieces of decorative paper; one slightly smaller than the piece on the cover, the second slightly smaller than that. Layer and glue the second piece onto the cover of the armoire.

Figure out the arrangement of the third paper and the decorative pieces for the front. Place the two crackled, decorative moldings at the top of the front with half a paper doily. Glue the third piece of paper based on this arrangement.

Use another half of a paper doily and glue to the front of the white paper doily.

16 Cut small pieces of decorative paper to adhere to the bottom of the layered paper.

17 Glue down the remaining decorative wood moldings: Add the wooden crackled flower to the top and the doorknob to the center right of the door.

18 String a decorative bead on a ribbon and tie it around the doorknob.

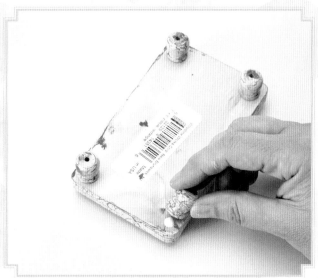

19 Glue the four feet onto the crackled wooden base, one in each corner. Allow the glue to dry.

20 Sand the edges of the base to give it a distressed look.

21 Glue the armoire box to the base.

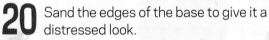

Tip

Be sure not to glue the door to the base or you won't be able to open your armoire!
If you don't want to make the whole armoire from scratch, visit the wood section of a craft store to find ready-made armoires.

createmixedmedia.com/paper-dolls

The Perfect Worn Leather Suitcase

Emilee didn't have to go far to find this butter-soft suitcase. Francesca's family had several stashed away in the attic of their Tuscan home. When Emilee admired this one, it was promptly gifted to her. How lucky can a girl be?

Nothing says "Italy" like soft, supple leather. I knew when I started this book that I would need a suitcase to store paper goodies in. I wanted it to look old and have vintage travel stickers stuck to it as reminders of good times that were had by its original owner.

Years ago, when I worked for a high-end handbag maker, I made these cute little handbags as Christmas presents to my co-workers. I tucked sweet notes and gift cards inside for the recipients. I enlarged the pattern a bit and found paper that resembled old leather and voilà—I had my old suitcase!

MATERIALS LIST

⅛" (3mm) wide double-sided tape

black ribbon, 12" (30 cm)

brown Glimmer Mist

die-cut minitags

flower stencil

glue stick

hole punch

metal keyhole

pencil

rhinestones in the shape of upholstery tacks

rustic key and tag

sandpaper or paper distresser

scissors

scrap of crochet lace

string

suitcase template

scrapbook paper

travel-themed washi tape and stickers

Tip

You will find a template for the suitcase in the back of this book. Or go to createmixedmedia.com/paper-dolls to print the template.

1 Trace the suitcase template on brown paper that resembles leather; be sure to include the side gussets. Cut out the template pieces. Lightly spray brown Glimmer Mist through a flower stencil onto the paper pieces.

2 Distress the paper with a distressing tool or sandpaper in random spots to make the "leather" show signs of aging.

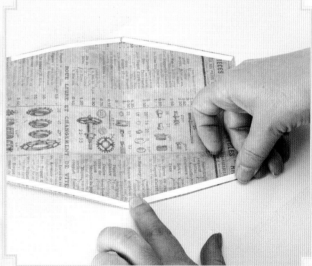

3 Score the fold lines on the suitcase and fold them toward you.

4 Fold the gussets in half with the "leather" sides facing each other. Tape the gussets to the inside of both sides of the suitcase using double-sided tape.

5 The narrower point of each gusset should be at the bottom of the bag so the bag opening will be wider than the base of the bag.

6 Trim any excess pieces off the gussets as needed.

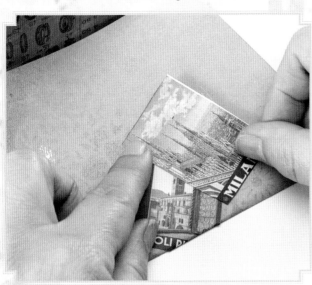

7 Adhere travel stickers or paper with a glue stick to the front of the suitcase.

8 Trace the keyhole hardware onto a piece of darker brown leather-like paper. Cut it out.

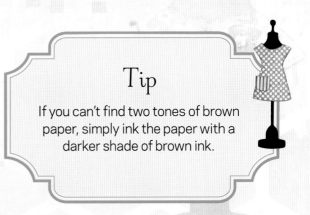

Tip

If you can't find two tones of brown paper, simply ink the paper with a darker shade of brown ink.

9 Distress the edges of the keyhole paper and the flap of the suitcase to show the suitcase is well traveled.

10 Glue a piece of vintage-looking crochet lace to the underside of the flap. Glue the darker leather paper to the top of the flap. Glue the key hardware on top of the paper. Allow glued elements to dry.

11 Attach travel-themed washi tape to the gussets and front for added interest and security. Add rhinestones to the front of the suitcase.

12 Punch two holes in the back of the suitcase close to the top of the bag and string a black ribbon through the holes to add a handle. Tie the knots on the inside of the bag to conceal them.

13 Create a mini luggage tag with a tag-shaped die-cut and a rustic key; tie them together with a string and tie the tag and key to the black ribbon handle.

The Backstreets of Asia

Kyoko knows all the great spots for Asian antiques. Some of the best shops are hidden treasures tucked along the backstreets of the downtown areas. Emilee was looking for a box to tuck away all of her tiny souvenirs.

Remember my memories of all the trinket shops in Chinatown? This is how I envision shops in Asia. The marketplaces overflow with paper lanterns, parasols and other goodies that tourists find irresistible. My family has traveled to southeast Asia several times, and I have lots of those goodies and love to find new ways to display them or use them in art projects.

This little trinket box was inspired by all of the little treasures we seem to collect on our journeys. It is a mini-version of a box to put dolls, umbrellas, chopsticks, a teacup or anything else that might be picked up along one's travels.

Starting with a small wooden box that can be found in any craft store, I used beautiful Asian-themed papers to make this. It would be equally as nice to hold small pieces of jewelry you may pick up on your travels.

MATERIALS LIST

4 wooden ball knobs, 1" (3cm)

acrylic paint: royal blue, black, gold metallic

Asian ephemera: coin, parasol, etc.

craft glue

decoupage medium

embellishments: paper flowers, trinkets

paintbrushes

scissors

scrapbook paper: Asian-themed, pink

wooden box, 6" × 4½" × 1" (15cm × 11cm × 3cm)

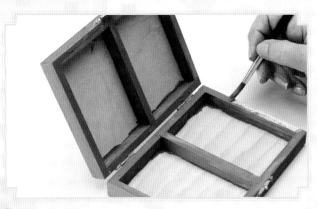

1 Paint the wooden box with royal blue acrylic paint. Leave the inside top and bottom panels unpainted.

2 Cut a rectangle out of an Asian-themed paper. It should be ½" (1cm) smaller than the edges of the top of the box. Cut two more pieces of different Asian-themed papers, each about 2½" × 3½" (6cm × 9cm).

3 Using decoupage medium, glue the papers to the box, overlapping slightly.

4 Cut two Japanese lanterns out of a fourth Asian-themed paper. Layer the lanterns on top of the box and adhere with decoupage medium. Embellish the box with paper flowers, trinkets and pink scrapbook paper. Adhere with craft glue.

5 On the right side of the lid, distress the edges of the second layer of paper by peeling it up slightly.

6 Open the box and cut decorative paper pieces to fit the inside nooks of the box lid and bottom. Adhere the papers with decoupage medium.

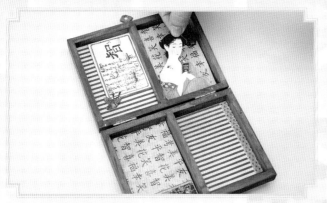

7 Layer smaller pieces of decorative paper in the nooks to simulate ephemera that Emilee may have collected in Asia. Adhere with decoupage medium.

8 Embellish the box with even more bits and bobs from Emilee's travels: an Asian parasol, an Asian coin, etc. Adhere with craft glue.

9 Paint four wooden knobs with black acrylic paint. Let the paint dry completely.

10 Glue a knob (flat side down) into each of the four corners of the box to create feet. Allow the glue to dry.

11 Using a dry brush and gold metallic paint, paint gold streaks along the feet and the sides of the box.

12 Coat the feet and sides of the box with decoupage medium to seal the gold paint.

5

Let's Play Dress Up!

createmixedmedia.com/paper-dolls

Time to Play!

Playing dress up is a part of every child's world from the time we are born until, well, forever. It's something we seem to never tire of. Costumes, evening wear and wedding gowns were always the crème de la crème of the fashion doll and paper doll world. I remember gasping in awe at the wedding gown that was on the last page of almost every paper doll book I had.

Therefore, it's just a given that I would transform some of my dolls with glorious costumes in the following projects. I will show you how to alter hairstyles, create a flouncy skirt or simply add wings to transform your paper dolls into something special.

Whether it's a canvas that you can display in a room or a mini-book to display on your nightstand, I'm sure you will find your inner child as you start to create these delightful costumes and perhaps think of some of your own.

createmixedmedia.com/paper-dolls

Fairy Book

Charley loves to read stories about fairies dancing around the English countryside, wearing the most delicate of dresses. I've always wanted to make a mini-book of fairy gowns, and when I spotted this odd-shaped chipboard book, I knew it would be perfect! If you can't find a ready-made book like this, it is easy to make one yourself because of its simple shapes. I love how each page layers on top of the next and you get a tiny peek of what's coming.

When creating a book like this, I encourage you to let your imagination go crazy. Grab a spare pair of wings, perhaps something extra glittery for dress up—crowns, flowers, fairy dust—these all belong within the pages of a fairy book! Shop your local craft store and find all sorts of pretty embellishments to inspire you.

MATERIALS LIST

- 12" (30cm) of pink ribbon
- assorted embellishments: charms, ribbons, bows
- assorted paper flowers
- binder rings, 2
- black Distress ink pad
- black fine-point pen
- blue cardstock
- brown chalk-ink edger
- brown Glimmer Mist
- Charley doll cutout and clothes
- chipboard book
- craft glue

- cream-colored tulle, 5½" × 8" (14cm × 20cm)
- crochet trim
- decorative paper punch
- die-cut angel wings
- die-cut fairy wing, crown and ticket
- double-sided tape
- English-themed scrapbook paper
- flower stencil
- gesso
- glue stick
- hole punch

- metal keyhole
- paintbrushes
- pencil
- punchinella
- rhinestone
- scissors
- script and other assorted stamps
- script washi tape
- small brown bag (found at any craft store)
- small decorative paperclip
- wooden button

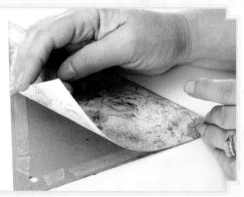

1 Cut a piece of scrapbook paper the same size and shape as the book cover. Punch holes in it, matching the placement of the holes in the chipboard cover. Repeat with a different patterned paper for the inside of the book cover. Ink the edges of the paper with the brown chalk-ink edger. Adhere them to both sides of the chipboard using double-sided tape or a tape runner. Trim any excess paper from the edges.

2 Cut out the Charley doll, a dress and accessories using the tank dress, pocket and headband templates designed for Charley. Add a contrasting ruffle to the bottom of the dress. Ink the edges of the doll and the dress using the brown chalk-ink edger. Glue the clothes onto the doll and glue the die-cut angel wings to her back.

3 Glue a piece of crochet trim to the edge of the inside of the book. Flip the cover over and place Charley where you'd like her to be. Mark holes with a pencil in the crook of her arm.

4 Punch holes through all the layers on those marks. Attach the doll to the cover by threading a pink ribbon through the holes and around her body. Tie the ribbon in a bow.

5 Embellish the right corner with a keyhole, and a paper flower (sprayed lightly with brown Glimmer Mist to make it look more vintage), gluing them with craft glue.

6 Cut a piece of blue cardstock (customized to the size of your book). Decorate the edge with a decorative paper punch. Place a floral stencil on the cardstock and mist it lightly with brown Glimmer Mist. Allow the mist to dry. Brush gesso in random places using the punchinella for a stencil.

7 Stamp a script stamp using black Distress ink on the brown bag. Write a saying on the bag using a black fine-point pen. Use decorative washi tape to adhere it to the middle of the blue cardstock.

8 Tie the strip of tulle in a knot. Glue the paper flower in the bottom left corner using craft glue, and glue the tulle slightly behind the flower. Add a rhinestone to the center of the flower. Trim the tulle as needed.

9 Clip a fairy wing to the right side of the brown bag using a small decorative paperclip. Slip a die-cut crown and a ticket into the bag. Punch two holes in the left side of the page to line up with the holes in the cover.

10 Trim a piece of decorative paper to the size and shape of a chipboard book page. Use a glue stick to adhere the paper to the chipboard. Ink the edges using a brown chalk-ink edger. Punch holes in the chipboard to match the blue page and the cover. Stamp the same script stamp in black distress ink along the right edge of the page.

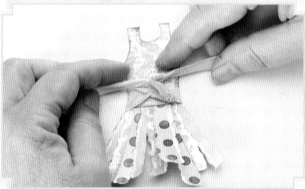

11 Trace the tank dress template onto scrapbook paper and cut it off just below the waist so you have the top half. Ink the edges. Using the same patterned paper, tear three strips of paper about ½" × 2" (1cm × 5cm).

12 Rip more strips of paper of the same size from contrasting paper. Glue the top of each piece of paper to the back of the bottom of the dress to create a skirt. The hemline should be uneven. Take a 10" (25cm) piece of rayon ribbon, spritz it with water and scrunch it up to make it wrinkly. Tie it in a knot around the waist of the dress

13 Paperclip the completed dress on the page. Add more embellishments as desired. Tie a bow through a wooden button using thread. Glue the button and some paper flowers to the page.

14 Complete more pages as desired. Bind all of the pages together with embellished binder rings. Use charms, ribbons and bows to embellish the binder clips.

Venetian Ball

Strolling down the streets of Venice, Francesca can't help but wonder what it would've been like to attend a Venetian ball in past times. The streets are lined with shop windows filled with ornate masks and the most intricate costumes. The old palaces that line the canals have ornate, gilded ballrooms that no doubt were the settings for such extravaganzas long ago.

This is one of my absolute favorite projects! The background was an experiment that turned out well, and I have used it many times since. Outside of my neighborhood sits a house with an outside wall with no windows facing the street. It's one of those houses that I'm sure everyone winces at because it's not in the best shape. Everyone except me, that is. The wall is the loveliest shade of brown with white and cream paint rolled over in areas, giving it a very uneven appearance. Perhaps they were covering graffiti. In any event, I love the texture; it reminds me of an old European building that hasn't been painted in years. I would do anything to create this effect on a wall inside my house!

MATERIALS LIST

⅛" (3mm) wooden dowel
4 patterns of Italian-themed paper
8" × 8" (20cm × 20cm) wrapped canvas
acrylic paints: burnt sienna, raw umber, metallic gold, chocolate, cream, brown
brown colored pencil
brown Glimmer Mist
chalk-ink edger in dark brown
decoupage medium
embellishments: flowers, rhinestones, ribbon
Francesca doll cutout
gesso
glue
paintbrushes
punchinella
scissors
scrap of chipboard
stencil (leaf or floral pattern)
Venetian ball gown template

1 Paint the canvas, including the sides, with a layer of chocolate brown paint. Let the paint dry completely.

2 Using a dry brush, brush on a light layer of gesso. Brush across the board first, then brush down to create a linen-like weave in the brushstrokes. Be sure to cover the sides with gesso as well.

Tip

You will find a template for the Venetian ball gown in the back of this book. Or go to createmixedmedia.com/paper-dolls to print the template. To speed up drying time, use a heat gun or a hair dryer.

3 Using cream-colored paint, stencil a leaf pattern in the upper right-hand corner. Stencil another leaf pattern in the upper left corner, running off the canvas. Add another area of stenciling in the bottom right-hand corner.

4 Cut out the Francesca doll. Cut off the bottom right part of her hair to give her an updo hairstyle. Don't worry about cutting out the doll's legs; they will eventually be cut off the bottom of the canvas.

5 Using the Venetian ball gown template, cut out pieces of Italian-themed paper to create the bottom of Francesca's dress. Cut out the bow and sash to Francesca's dress using a fourth paper. Ink the edges of the dress and the bow using the chalk-ink edger

6 Draw the lines of the creases of the bow using a brown colored pencil.

7 Arrange the pieces on the canvas to make sure they fit. Apply decoupage medium to the canvas, not the paper. Place the pieces of paper down to adhere. Cover each piece of paper with a layer of decoupage medium to secure it. Apply the doll first, then start with the outside pieces of the dress. The very middle piece should be last. Then apply the sash and the bow so they cover the top pieces of the dress.

Tip

Don't worry about the top pieces meeting perfectly; the sash of her bow will cover those up.

8 Using burnt sienna, raw umber and metallic gold, paint Francesca's hair to simulate an upswept hairstyle. Be sure to add paint to all of the hair on the doll for a cohesive look. Finally, using metallic gold, add highlights to her hair. Let dry. Brush a coat of decoupage medium over the whole canvas, including the sides. Let the medium dry completely.

9 Block the part of the doll and canvas that you want to protect. Spray brown Glimmer Mist through punchinella in random places on the canvas. Allow the Glimmer Mist to dry.

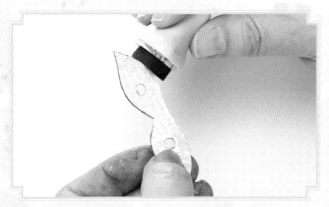

10 Glue a piece of decorative paper to a piece of chipboard. Trace the eye mask template on the double layer and cut it out. Punch small holes for the eyes. Ink the edges of the mask using the brown chalk-ink edger.

11 Glue a ⅛" (3mm) wooden dowel to the back of the mask. Adhere a flower and a jewel embellishment to the front of the mask. Tie a piece of brown ribbon into a bow and adhere it beneath the flower.

12 Arrange the mask and other flower and rhinestone embellishments on the canvas. Adhere each using a dot of glue.

13 Lightly mist a paper flower with water and crumple it up. Glue it to Francesca's hair as an adornment.

Joy Canvas

Kyoko might adore her crazy mixed-up clothes but, every so often, she likes the calmness of a traditional Asian look. (You could make a beautiful kimono for this piece if you'd like.)

My inspiration for this piece was simply the color red. I hardly use red at all and I wasn't sure what other colors to use, so I did something I rarely do: Without thinking, I picked out colors that I would not normally put together. Instead of going with the cutesy colors of the outfit, I chose not-so-cutesy colors that were not an obvious match for the papers I was using. I absolutely love the result. I also pulled out my neglected sewing machine for this project and stitched around some mulberry paper, creating another element for my piece. I totally recommend getting outside your comfort zone and challenging yourself with new colors or techniques. You may end up with a combination you really love.

MATERIALS LIST

8" × 10" (20cm × 25cm) canvas board

acrylic paints: cream, medium brown, teal, royal blue

black marker

brown chalk-ink edger

brown Glimmer Mist

brown scrapbook paper

craft glue

decoupage medium

embellishments: Asian-themed button and coins, paper rose

gesso

Kyoko cutout and clothes templates

metal photo corner holder

mulberry paper with gold thread embedded in it

paintbrushes

paper distresser

punchinella

red colored pencil

red ink pad

red thread

scissors

several Asian-themed scrapbook papers

sewing machine

stamp, Asian characters

umbrella template

Tip

You will find a template for the umbrella in the back of this book. Or go to createmixedmedia.com/paper-dolls to print the template.

1 Cover an 8" × 10" (20cm × 25cm) canvas board with a layer of cream-colored acrylic paint. Allow to dry.

2 Add teal, medium brown and royal blue in random places. Begin to blend each paint with the next but don't overmix. Allow to dry completely.

Tip

In a canvas such as this, where the center area will eventually be covered with collage elements, use that place to practice mixing the paint and getting brushstrokes that are pleasing to you.

3 Using a dry brush, apply a thin layer of gesso vertically. Then brush horizontally to create crosshatching lines.

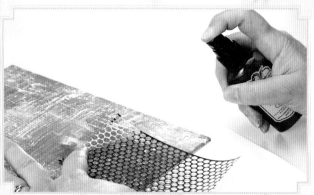

4 Place a piece of punchinella on the canvas and spray with brown Glimmer Mist in random areas.

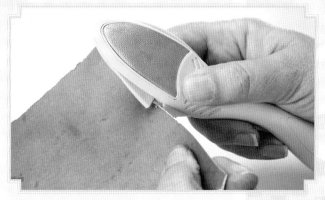

5 Cut a piece of brown scrapbook paper to 5¼" × 8" (13cm × 20cm) and distress the edges with a paper distresser.

6 Adhere the paper to the center of the canvas using decoupage medium. Be careful not to adhere the edges too tightly.

7 Peel and tear the edges of the paper to make it look even more distressed. If you don't have a paper distresser, use a pair of scissors as you would to curl ribbon.

8 Cut a piece of Asian-themed scrapbook paper into a 4" × 6¾" (10cm × 17cm) rectangle. Take a piece of mulberry paper with gold thread and rip it to a size that is slightly smaller than the rectangle. Stamp Asian characters with red ink, slightly off center, on the mulberry paper.

9 Starting in the upper right corner, sew the mulberry paper to the scrapbook paper using red thread. The lines should not be even or perfect. Leave the threads hanging.

10 Place a metal photo corner holder on the lower right corner and squeeze the metal together to clasp it to the piece.

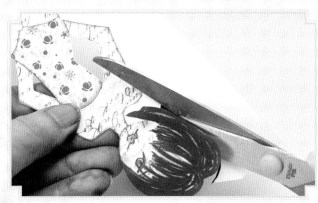

11 Place a dot of glue on the metal photo corner and cover the back of the paper with a layer of decoupage medium. Press the paper onto the brown paper.

12 Cut out the Kyoko doll and trim her hair to give her an asymmetrical hairstyle.

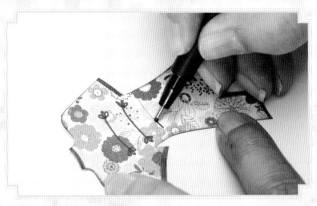

13 Using Kyoko's templates, trace and cut a pair of pants, a shirt and a headband from scrapbook papers. Ink all edges with a brown chalk-ink edger and edge the shirt with a red colored pencil. Using a black marker, draw Asian shirt closures. Glue the clothes to the Kyoko doll.

14 Cut the pieces for the umbrella using the umbrella template and alternate each panel with a different pattern of scrapbook paper. Ink the edges of each piece with the brown chalk-ink edger.

Tip

Hold the clothes over the doll to see if you need to trim any edges before gluing.

createmixedmedia.com/paper-dolls

15 Glue the pieces of the umbrella together, overlapping the pieces ever so slightly. Create a point at the tip of the umbrella and trim if neccessary.

16 Paint a coat of decoupage medium on the back of the umbrella. Place the umbrella in the lower left corner and press to adhere. Layer decoupage medium on the back of the doll and place her legs slightly overlapping the umbrella and the mulberry paper.

17 Embellish the upper right-hand corner of the sewn paper with Asian-themed buttons, coins and paper roses. Adhere each item with a drop of craft glue.

createmixedmedia.com/paper-dolls

Friendship Chain

What paper doll book would be complete without a paper doll chain? These are so much fun to make! I have several in my studio, dancing along the walls. They've ended up as cards and look adorable decorating large packages. Dress them up in Valentine's Day or Halloween outfits or their holiday best and decorate your mantel. They make wonderful party decorations and favors. I could go on and on, but I think you get the idea, and you will, no doubt, come up with your own ideas for these cuties!

MATERIALS LIST

6 small brads, 2 large brads

assorted scrapbook papers

brown chalk-ink edger

colored pencils

craft glue or glue stick

decorative paper with a script design

fine-point Sharpie marker, black

flower die cuts

gold marker

hole punch

paper doll chain template (3 dolls) and 3 outfit templates

scissors

Tip
You will find templates for the paper dolls in **Chapter 2**.

1 Trace the paper doll chain templates onto decorative paper to create three paper dolls. Draw in their eyes and hair with a fine-point Sharpie. Color in the eyes and lips with colored pencils of your choice. Shade the eyelids in a brown tone. Color in the hair using three shades of brown for a natural effect. Color the hair in the direction you would comb the hair. Using a gold marker, add a strand of hair for added texture.

2 Color the shoes using a black marker.

Tip

Your dolls don't have to have faces.

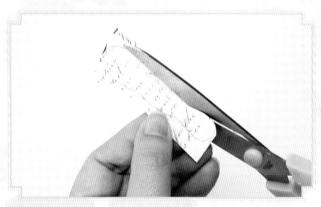

3 Cut out each doll and her outfit, including the arms and legs.

4 Ink the edges of the clothes and each body part. Punch holes in the places indicated on the templates (both ends of the arms, the shoulders of the dolls, their clothes and the center of each of the two flowers).

5 Embellish each dress with matching pockets and ruffles using glue.

6 Add headbands, bows and flowers to the dolls' heads.

7 Line up the holes on the dress, the doll's shoulder and an arm. Bind them together using a colorful brad that matches the dress. Continue attaching arms and clothing to each doll.

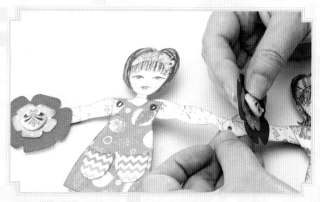

8 Attach a die-cut flower to two dolls' hands, thereby connecting two dolls together, using a large decorative brad. Attach the third doll to one of the other dolls in the same way.

9 Shade the dolls' cheeks using a rosy red colored pencil.

6

Are You Ready to Go on a Journey?

don't let your dreams fly away

DREAMS

The ideas seemed endless when I chose a travel theme for this book. The world is full of inspiration! Countries seem to have a special feeling all their own, don't they? For me, France conjures thoughts of fabulous art, cathedrals, acres of lavender fields, and vineyards with their endless rows of grapevines. High-end couture, little black dresses and signature perfumes also come to mind.

When thinking of England, tea parties, royalty, fairies and medieval times are among my first thoughts. But then there's also the 1960s London with miniskirts, go-go boots and frosted lipsticks. This was the fashion capital for free spirits in the sixties. There are so many possibilities when you consider an English theme!

I envision walking through the woods of Europe, thick with trees. You know, those forests where the best fairy tales took place. Think of the serene countryside of Tuscany, its rolling green hills with sprawling Italian villas perched on top. Or perhaps villages high on the cliffs overlooking the rugged coastline of the Mediterranean Sea.

With Asia, I think of bright colors like those in a set of origami papers. Intricate kimonos, lanterns and fortune cookies are just a handful of images that tease the imagination. A stroll through Chinatown and its colorful shops is all one needs to find inspiration.

This was all my inspiration for the next few projects. Whether it's a place you imagine going to or perhaps just walking through your favorite craft store and finding yourself attracted to a certain paper, I know you'll find a lot of inspiration for many projects to use with your paper dolls. I hope you have as much fun making these projects as I did.

Into the Woods Shadow Box

When creating Charley and her mod world, I couldn't help but think of traditional England. I think of kings and queens, castles and green, misty forests where fairy tales take place. It was difficult to give up these images, but when I saw this paper with the trees, I knew I wanted to create a bit of the English countryside in a project.

I was so attracted to this paper of abstract trees. I immediately thought of cutting it up and layering the trees in a shadow box frame, using lots of layers to create the forest. The wonderful part of this project is if you can't find a paper similar to this, you can create your own trees by cutting the simple shapes from coordinating papers and layering them on a plain background. A shadow box is the perfect place to rest a paper doll. You can create any kind of scene you like in any size frame for a very special gift.

MATERIALS LIST

3D adhesive dots or double-sided tape pieces

8" × 10" (20cm × 25cm) shadow box

assorted scrapbook papers

brown and light yellow markers

brown chalk-ink edger

brown or black colored paper

craft glue

Design Your Own Doll template

multiple scrapbook papers with trees or snowflakes

owl die cut

paintbrush

pencil

punchinella

red button

scissors

snowflake buttons

white acrylic paint

Tip

You will find Design Your Own Doll templates in **Chapter 2** Or go to createmixedmedia.com/paper-dolls to print the templates.

1 Glue the shadow box description paper to a piece of scrapbook paper with trees on it. This will provide a sturdy substrate for the rest of the items in the shadow box.

2 Draw three tree trunks and branches on two different kinds of patterned paper. Cut them out and match their height to the size of your shadow box. Draw them in various sizes. Ink the edges of the trees using the brown chalk-ink edger. Layer the first two trees on the substrate using 3D adhesive dots or tape squares. On the first tree, use one layer of 3D tape. Give the second tree more dimension by stacking two pieces of 3D tape together.

3 Cut out a doll using the Design Your Own Doll template. Give the doll hair by coloring with brown and light yellow markers. I chose not to draw a face on this doll, but you certainly can if you'd like. Ink the knee and neck area of the doll. The rest of her will be covered by a coat, hat and boots that you can cut out of scrapbook paper that coordinates with your background.

4 Ink the edges of her clothes and draw in the details using a brown or black colored pencil (the coat opening, where the sleeves are, the brim of the hat, etc.). Glue the clothes on the doll and a red button on the coat. Set aside for later.

5 Using white acrylic paint and a punchinella, randomly place dots on the trees and the substrate to create a snowy effect.

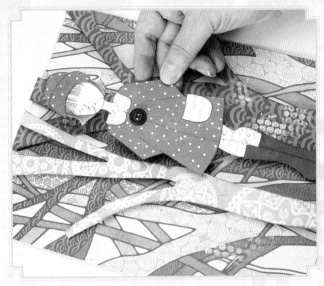

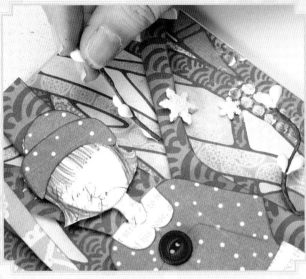

6 Attach the doll to the substrate using 3D adhesive dots.

7 Glue on snowflake buttons in random places. Using white snow floral picks, put a dot of craft glue at the bottom and tuck them behind the trees. Add an owl cutout to the back layer of trees.

8 Tuck the third tree between the glass and the frame of the shadow box.

9 Place the substrate back in the frame and secure it in place.

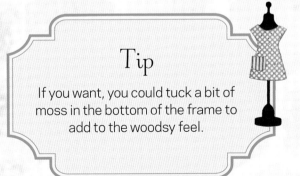

Tip

If you want, you could tuck a bit of moss in the bottom of the frame to add to the woodsy feel.

createmixedmedia.com/paper-dolls

French Banner

Creating anything French is just, well, plain yummy. I've been enthralled with all things French for years. I seem to snap up anything with French script or an Eiffel Tower on it and it has been a huge inspiration in my artwork. With this banner I tried to capture the essence of all things French with the colors, the beautiful millinery quality of the flowers and the pale pink ribbon that ties it all together. This banner just oozes yumminess.

How fun it would be to make this for a young girl's room with her name on it? I made one for my guest room and I can't wait to hang it up! I may even add a few more banners just to lengthen it a bit. Yes, that will give me yet another excuse to create more paper dolls!

You can hunt down all those pieces of vintage lace and buttons you've been hoarding. You know the stuff I'm talking about. And just when you think you've added enough goodies, add one more piece!

MATERIALS LIST

¼" (6mm) hole punch

alphabet stickers

Belle and Francesca dolls, clothes and templates

brown chalk-ink edger

brown Glimmer Mist

buttons (one should be heart-shaped)

chipboard flower

craft glue

distresser

embellishments: paper flowers, wired rose with the stem curled, lace flower, rhinestones

glue stick

paper doilies, white and colored

pink ribbon, 2 yards (183cm)

pink threads

scalloped scissors

scissors

scrapbook paper in a variety of French themes

1 Cut three triangles (the two longer sides will be 8½" (22cm) and the top will be 6¼" (16cm) out of three different French-themed scrapbook papers. Cut a strip of paper in a different pattern that is the length of the top of the triangle. Trim the bottom edge of this strip with scalloped scissors and ink the edge. Score a line down the center of the strip. Fold the paper over the top of one of the triangles and glue it down front and back. Trim the edges of the folded paper to match the angle of the triangle. Ink the edges of the whole triangle. Repeat for the two remaining triangles.

2 Glue a small paper doily in the center of the triangle. Layer a smaller doily on the first doily and glue it down using a glue stick.

3 Cut a banner out of French script paper . The banner should be 3" × 1" (8 cm × 3cm) with an inverted **V** at the bottom. Ink the edges with the brown chalk-ink edger. Then cut two more banners, each slightly smaller than the first. Use a contrasting paper from the first banner. Ink the edges.

4 Double thread the holes of one button and tie a knot. Trim the ends of the thread. Repeat with the second button.

5 Arrange the paper flower, lace flower, wire-stemmed flower, banners and buttons in a pleasing arrangement on the paper doilies. Glue each piece to the paper using craft glue.

6 Using letter stickers, add the word *amour* to the larger banner. Then repeat steps 1 through 3 on the remaining two triangles.

7 Lightly spray a paper doily with brown Glimmer Mist and cut it in half.

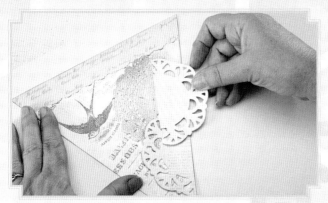

8 Ink the edges of two contrasting colored paper doilies. Ink the edges and cut in half. Arrange one half of each doily on one triangle and glue it down.

9 Distress the edges of a chipboard flower and ink the edges with the brown chalk-ink edger.

10 Arrange the embellishments (chipboard flower, paper flowers, buttons, banner and rhinestones) in a pleasing manner and glue them on top of the doilies to cover the edges.

11 Spray the triangle lightly with brown Glimmer Mist. Wipe the button with a paper towel to remove the excess Glimmer Mist if needed.

12 Cut out the Belle doll and her pants. Trace dress and headband templates onto coordinating paper. Cut them out and ink the edges. Glue the clothes and a button onto the doll. Glue the doll onto the side of the triangle opposite the embellishments.

Repeat steps 7–12 for the remaining banner on the final triangle in a mirror image. Use Francesca for this triangle.

13 Punch holes in the top of each triangle, about 1" (3cm) from each end. String the three triangles together using a pink ribbon.

don't let your dreams fly awa

DREAMS

Under the Tuscan Sunshine

I'm not sure there are a lot of clotheslines in Tuscany. But I, for one, choose to imagine there are! I imagine Francesca picking the herbs and ripe vegetables out of the garden, right outside the kitchen, for the day's lunch. Next to the garden would be a charming old clothesline with colorful dresses fluttering in the wind with perhaps some tall cypress trees in the far distance. I believe there might even be an easel standing near those trees with a half-finished painting sitting on it. Yep, as I create paper dolls, I find it so easy to come up with stories to go with them!

I believe this was my first piece for this book. I wasn't even sure how it would fit in, but I have always wanted to create a clothesline with paper clothes and this was the time to do it. The background was so much fun to do, making lots of layers, using paint and my favorite stencils. Using embellishments, such as the clothespin poles to tie into the theme, came to me in the middle of the night as many of my ideas do. The distressed finish added just the right vintage touch.

MATERIALS LIST

2 wooden clothespins with a crackle finish

4 mini-clothespins

8" × 10" (20cm × 25cm) wrapped canvas

acrylic paints: cream, teal, medium brown, white

assorted scrapbook paper

brown chalk-ink edger

craft glue

decoupage medium

embellishments: wooden tag, flowers, rhinestones, resin tile, word stickers, buttons, etc.

fine-point pen, black

floral stencil

gesso

Glimmer Mist, brown

linen weave stencil

natural colored string

paintbrushes

reversed chicken-wire stencil

ribbon

water spritzer

1 Paint a basecoat of cream acrylic paint. Include the sides of the canvas. While the cream paint is wet, brush in some teal paint using random strokes. Don't forget the sides! Allow to dry or speed up the drying process with a hair dryer or heat gun.

2 Brush in some medium brown acrylic paint in random areas. Let this dry completely.

Tip
Be light-handed with the paint.
Allow the paint to dry.

113

3 Place the floral stencil in random places on the canvas and paint through it with white paint.

4 Using a small amount of cream paint, lightly mist the canvas with water and spread it thinly over the whole canvas to tone down the color. Allow to dry.

5 Drybrush gesso on the canvas in random places. Allow this to dry. Place a reversed chicken wire stencil in random places and paint through it with medium brown acrylic paint. Allow the paint to dry.

6 Place the linen weave stencil in random places near the center of the canvas. Paint through it with medium brown. Allow this to dry.

7 Layer a coat of decoupage medium on the canvas and the sides. Let it dry. While the canvas is drying, tie the natural colored string around the tops of the two clothespins to connect them. Determine the length of the string by positioning the clothespins on the canvas, about 1" (3cm) from either edge.

8 Using craft glue, adhere the clothespins. I chose to have the right clothespin slightly lower than the left.

Tip

Wipe the excess paint off your stencils while you're waiting for the canvas to dry.

9 Embellish the bottom corners of the canvas with flowers, string, rhinestones, word stickers and other trinkets. Glue them to the canvas using craft glue.

10 In the right corner, glue a piece of floral paper. Slide part of the paper under the clothespin. Finish embellishing the right corner with more flowers, buttons and stickers.

11 Spray brown Glimmer Mist in both bottom corners.

12 Trace the clothes templates onto scrapbook paper and cut them out. Ink the edges with a brown chalk-ink edger. Then glue the pocket and the pleat to the clothes.

13 Attach the dress and skirt to the clothesline with mini-clothespins, and tie the wooden tag onto the clothesline with the ribbon.

Choose a saying and write it across the top of the canvas, following the sweep of the clothesline.

Tip

To avoid getting a lot of glue on your hands, put a dot of glue on a piece of scrap paper and dip small embellishments like buttons and rhinestones in the glue.

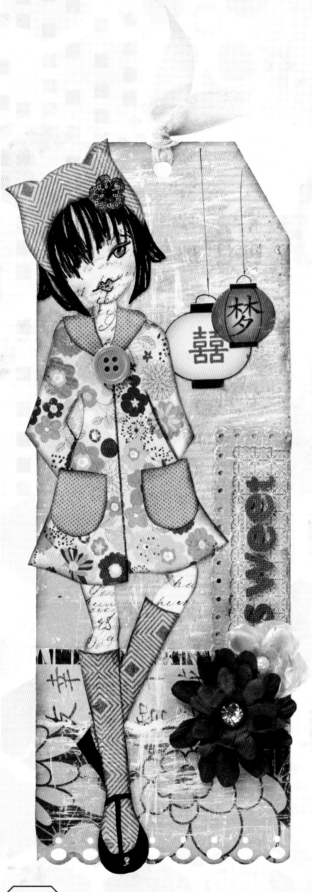

Harajuku Tags

I love these oversized tags. They make a charming substitute for a card, or you can hang one from a gift bag containing a special treasure. I must admit there are times when the gift tags are better than the goodies inside! Any one of the paper dolls would look adorable on these, and there's plenty of room for lots of embellishments. How fun it would be to make a tag with a paper doll that looks like the recipient!

Don't limit yourself to any one style. These could be adorable Valentine's Day or holiday cards. I made some with gorgeous bride dolls that I attached to shower gifts. With all the themed embellishments available, let your imagination soar with these tags. But I must warn you … creating these tags can be addictive!

MATERIALS LIST

¼" (6mm) hole punch

alphabet stickers

Asian-themed scrapbook paper

black pen

brown cardstock

chalk-ink edger, brown

craft glue

embellishments: flowers, jewels

gesso

glue stick

Kyoko doll and her coat outfit; other paper dolls and outfits as desired

paintbrush

paper with an Asian lantern pattern

pink button

rayon ribbon

ruler

scalloped scissors

scissors

1 Cut out the Kyoko doll and the pieces to her coat. Ink the sides of the doll and her clothes with the brown chalk-ink edger.

2 Glue Kyoko's clothes onto the doll using a glue stick.

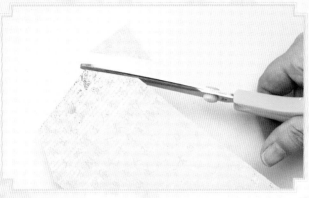

3 Using an Asian-themed paper, cut a 3½" × 9" (9cm × 23cm) rectangle. Cut off the top two corners at an angle and punch a hole in the top center.

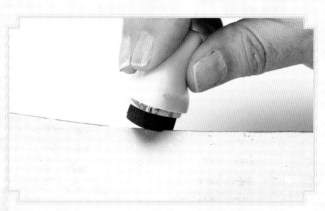

4 Ink the edges of the tag using the brown chalk-ink edger.

5 Layer two 3" (8cm) scraps of paper to the bottom of the tag using a glue stick. Here the bottom piece has a decorative edge at the bottom and is torn at the top.

6 Paint a light layer of gesso over the whole tag using a dry brush. Paint the gesso both horizontally and vertically on the tag to add texture.

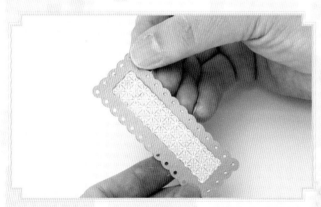

7 Cut a 3" (8cm) frame out of brown craft card-stock and scallop the edges. Layer a piece of pink paper underneath the frame and adhere with glue.

8 Glue the framed piece to the right edge of the tag. Allow part of the scalloped edge to hang over the edge of the tag.

9 Trim the edge of the frame that is hanging over the tag edge. Add a bit of gesso on top of the frame to grunge it up a bit. Ink the edge of the pink paper and the bottom layer. Cut out two lanterns from the lantern-patterned scrapbook paper.

10 Arrange the doll and the lanterns on the tag. Glue all the pieces to the tag down with a glue stick.

11 Using a black pen and a ruler, draw lines for the lanterns to hang from.

12 Add letter stickers to the pink and brown frame, spelling out a word of your choice. I chose the word *sweet*.

13 Place a dot of craft glue on each of the flower embellishments and attach them to the bottom of the frame. Add a jewel to the center of each flower. Place a pink button on Kyoko's coat.

14 Spray a piece of ribbon with water and crinkle it to give it a vintage feel. Lace the ribbon through the hole and tie a bow.

Tip

Allow some of your embellishments to hang over the edge of the tag for added interest.

The Perfect Worn Leather Suitcase Template

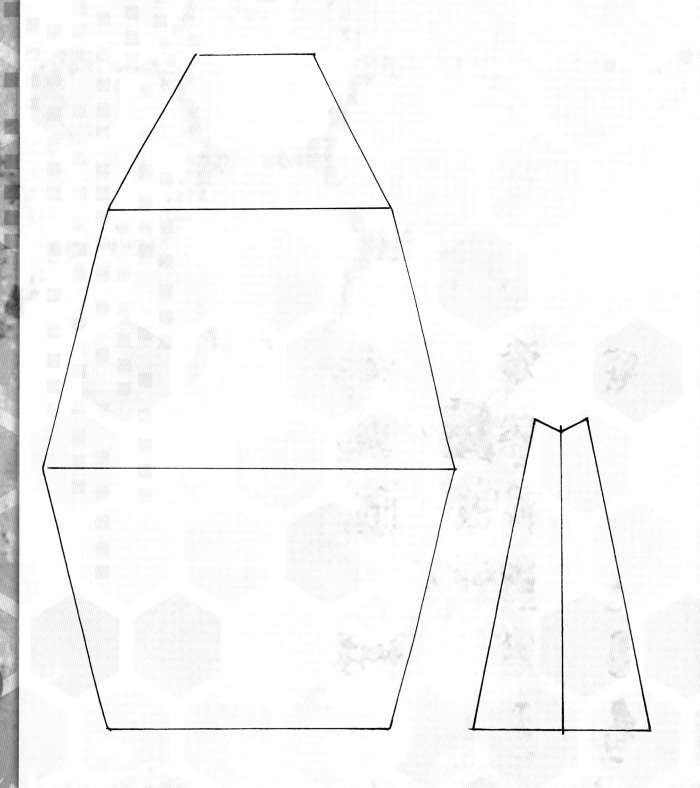

Emilee Goes to the Beach
Template

Pagoda in the Park Template

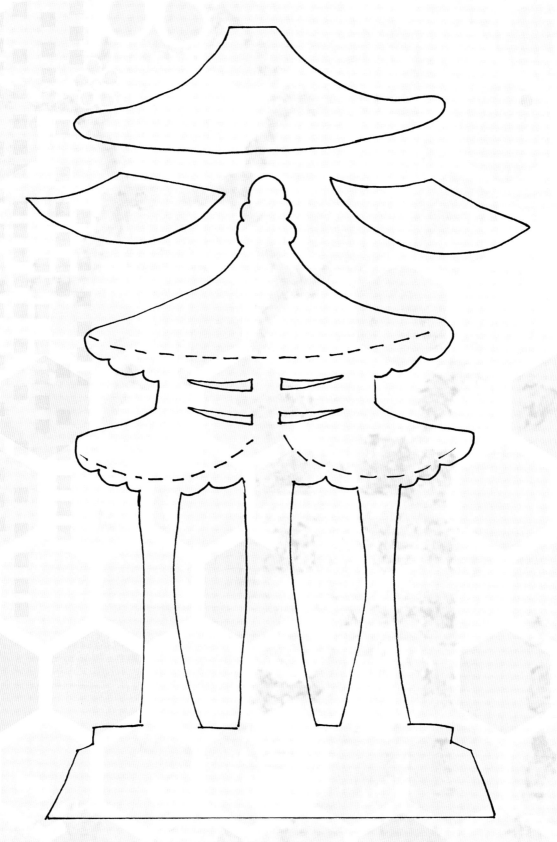

createmixedmedia.com/paper-dolls

The City of Light Template

Joy Canvas
Umbrella Template

Venetian Ball Template

Resources

Prima Marketing

primamarketinginc.com

embellishments, stamps, stencils, paper

My Minds Eye

mymindseye.com

embellishments, stamps, stencils, paper

Basic Grey

basicgrey.com

embellishments, paper, albums, tools

Splash of Color

splashofcolor.us

embellishments, paper, paint, tools, washi tape

Ranger

rangerink.com

embellishments, paper, paint, tools, ink

Mod Podge

plaidonline.com

decoupage medium, paint, embellishments, stamps, stencils, paper

The Crafters Workshop

thecraftersworkshop.com

stencils, dies

Tattered Angels

mytatteredangels.com

Glimmer Mist, paint

createmixedmedia.com/paper-dolls

Index

 Other fine North Light Books are available from your
favorite bookstore, art supply store or online supplier.
Visit our website at fwmedia.com.

18 17 16 15 14   5 4 3 2 1

Distributed in Canada by Fraser Direct
100 Armstrong Avenue
Georgetown, ON, Canada L7G 5S4
Tel: (905) 877-4411

Distributed in the U.K. and Europe
by F&W Media International LTD
Brunel House, Forde Close, Newton Abbot, TQ12 4PU, UK
Tel: (+44) 1626 323200, Fax: (+44) 1626 323319
Email: enquiries@fwmedia.com

Distributed in Australia by Capricorn Link
P.O. Box 704, S. Windsor NSW, 2756 Australia
Tel: (02) 4560-1600; Fax: (02) 4577 5288
Email: books@capricornlink.com.au

ISBN 13: 978-1-4403-2901-2

Edited by Kristy Conlin and Brittany VanSnepson
Designed by Elyse Schwanke
Photography by Christine Polomsky and Kris Kandler
Production coordinated by Jennifer Bass

Metric Conversion Chart

TO CONVERT	TO	MULTIPLY BY
Inches	Centimeters	2.54
Centimeters	Inches	0.4
Feet	Centimeters	30.5
Centimeters	Feet	0.03
Yards	Meters	0.9
Meters	Yards	1.1

createmixedmedia.com/paper-dolls

The eyes are the windows of the soul.

About the Author

Julie Nutting has been drawing fashion figures since she was nine years old. She brought the unique look of fashion illustration to the craft world in 2008 when she was first published in a national craft magazine. Her first book, *Collage Couture,* was well received in the mixed-media craft arena. Since then, she has created a top-selling product line with Prima Marketing, featuring her whimsical illustrations. She holds mixed-media classes throughout the world. She resides in sunny southern California with her husband and two spoiled fur babies.

Acknowledgments

To my mother who gave me the wonderful gift of paper dolls, many times over.

I must thank the most wonderful people, young and old who have taken my classes, read my books and purchased my products. You have touched me greatly. You have shared stories of your childhood, you have made art in honor of your mothers, and you have made paper dolls to pass the time in a nursing home. You have formed online and in-person groups to share your paper dolls. People from all over are introducing their children to paper dolls. You have all found your inner child, learned how to play again and truly inspire me!

Need More Couture in Your Life?

Receive FREE downloadable bonus materials (including templates!) when you visit:
CreateMixedMedia.com/paper-dolls.

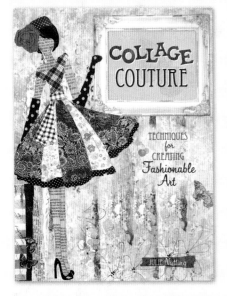

These and other fine North Light products are available at your favorite art & craft retailer, bookstore or online supplier.
Visit our website at **CreateMixedMedia.com**.

Find the latest issues of **Cloth Paper Scissors** on newsstands, or visit **ClothPaperScissors.com**.

 Follow **CreateMixedMedia.com** for the latest news, free wallpapers, free demos and chances to win FREE BOOKS!

Get Your Art in Print!

Visit **CreateMixedMedia.com** for up-to-date information on **Incite, Zen Doodle** and other North Light competitions.

Enter today for a chance to see your art in print!